SCHOLASTIC discover more™ stickers!

Dinosaurs

DO YOU THINK HE SAURUS?

Fill this prehistoric scene with your dinosaur stickers. But watch out!

Dino time

First there were little dinosaurs. They were small, but they were mean. They thrived, and more dinosaurs came along. Some got REALLY big. And REALLY mean. Dinosaurs ruled Earth for millions of years. Then, suddenly, they all died out.

251-199 MYA
Triassic

The Triassic period was hot and dry. Crocodiles, turtles, small dinos, and tiny mammals slunk and scuttled around.

WHAT FOLLOWED THE DINOSAURS?

Archaeopteryx

Compsognathus

Iguanadon

145-65 MYA
Cretaceou

Giganotosaurus

THEIR TAILS!

Spinosaurus

Pteranodon: a flying reptile

Dinosaurs lived between about 230 and 65 million years ago, in the Triassic, Jurassic, and Cretaceous time periods.

228 MYA

Herrerasaurus

Eoraptor

Coelophysis

Match the stickers to their shapes!

Diplodocus

Apatosaurus

Allosaurus

199-145 MYA
Jurassic

The Jurassic period was hot and wet. Forests sprung up, so plant-eating dinos got bigger. The meat-eating dinos that ate them got bigger, too.

Argentinosaurus

No one knows why the dinos died out. Maybe an asteroid hit Earth and changed its climate. Be glad! Giganotosaurus was a 40-foot-long killing machine with 8-inch teeth.

The Cretaceous period brought flowers and lots of feathered birds. What could possibly go wrong?

Tyrannosaurus rex

Velociraptor

Triceratops

-65 MYA-
the end
(for
dinosaurs)

WHAT DOES A DINOSAUR EAT FOR LUNCH?

WHO'S for dinner?

Argentinosaurus: herbivore

Many huge dinosaurs ate nothing but plants. It took a LOT of salad to fill up Argentinosaurus! Herbivores had to eat and eat and eat and eat and eat, pretty much 24/7.

magnolia flower

pinecones

cycad

moss

gingko leaves

redwood cone

fern

horsetail

pine branch

pebbles

berries

Corythosaurus weighed about 8,000 pounds—and ate only fruit and young leaves.

some herbivores swallowed stones to help grind up their food

4

Meat-eating dinos chomped on all kinds of meaty treats. Favorite food? The meat from dead animals. No running or fighting required.

BLOOD . . . OR KETCHUP?

ANYTHING IT WANTS!

small, furry mammal

turtle

other dinos

maggots

lizard

bug

frog

egg

fish

some carnivores were skilled fishers

Giganotosaurus: carnivore

Oviraptors were omnivores. They ate EVERYTHING!

Most carnivores were hunters AND scavengers, which means they ate the meat and bones of dead animals.

DIYdinosaurs

Hand-build a herbivore

LONG NECK ⬆
This will help reach those tender leaves at the very top of the tree.

NICE LEGS ⬆
Something has to hold up that big tummy.

Use stickers to dream up your very own dinosaur.

⬅ **BODY ARMOR**
Help your herbivore defend itself with a lashing tail, horns, or spikes. Do ya feel lucky, T. rex?

HELLO! MY NAME IS

| Vulcanodon | Amargasaurus | Ankylosaurus | Protoceratops | Diplodocus |

Create a carnivore

Velociraptor

HEADS UP!
A big head is good for head butting, and razor-sharp teeth make deadly bites.

STRONG TAIL
A long tail improves balance, and long back legs make a carnivore FAST. Run, little victims! Run!

TINY ARMS
Hands grip fleeing prey. (But short arms aren't good for push-ups!)

CLAWS
Sharp claws may help with slashing, tearing, slicing, and dicing.

HELLO! MY NAME IS

Carnotaurus   Compsognathus   Deinonychus   Eoraptor   Microraptor

7

Dino records

It wasn't OK for dinosaurs to be just average. To survive, they had to be the BIGGEST! The FASTEST! The TOOTHIEST! Here are some dinos that set amazing records.

WHAT'S AS BIG AS A DINO BUT WEIGHS NOTHING?

ITS SHADOW!

FIRST TO FLY
Archaeopteryx. This may have been the very first bird.

you are this big!

HEAVIEST MEAT-EATER
Giganotosaurus. It weighed 9 tons and was the heaviest carnivore EVER. Its brain was the shape of a banana.

BIGGEST EGG
A coelurosaur's. It was 17 inches long! Dino moms may have laid 20 eggs at a time—OUCH.

LONGEST MEAT-EATER
Spinosaurus. It was 52 feet long—that's like four cars lined up bumper to bumper. With a biting, snapping, hungry front end.

GULP!

MOST INTELLIGENT
Troödon. It had a big brain for its size. Troödon moms must have been very proud.

look out
for fun extra
stickers, to use
wherever you like!

USE YOUR STICKERS
TO COMPLETE
THE SCENES!

STICKERS
FOR
PAGE 1

Eoraptor

Archaeopteryx

Iguanadon

Herrerasaurus

Coelophysis

Allosaurus

Giganotosaurus

Diplodocus

Triceratops

STICKERS
FOR
PAGES 2–3

Tyrannosaurus rex

magnolia flower

pinecones

moss

small, furry mammal

maggots

pebbles

redwood cone

other dino

turtle

lizard

gingko leaves

horsetail

frog

egg

fish

STICKERS FOR PAGES 4-5

cycad

STICKERS FOR PAGES 6-7

dinosaur eggs

Archaeopteryx

Gallimimus

Microraptor

Troodon

STICKERS
FOR
PAGES 8-9

Stegosaurus

STICKERS
FOR
PAGES 10-11

STICKERS
FOR
PAGES 12–13

STICKERS
FOR
PAGES 14–15

YOU CAN'T GET AWAY, GALLIMIMUS. I LOVE FAST FOOD!

STRONGEST BITE ➡
Tyrannosaurus rex. Its bite was ten times stronger than an alligator's is. Deadliest bite from a land animal EVER.

LOOK OUT!

BIGGEST
Argentinosaurus. It was 115 feet long. Its shoulder blade was bigger than a car!

SMALLEST
Microraptor. It was 2.5 feet long and had four wings. FOUR!

FASTEST
Gallimimus. It could run 40 miles per hour—that's as fast as a racehorse. Its name means "chicken mimic."

LEAST INTELLIGENT
Stegosaurus. It had a huge body with a brain the size of a lime! People once thought it had an extra brain in its tail. It didn't.

brain this size

The MAIN

Who would win in a fight between Tyrannosaurus rex and Triceratops? You might be surprised. . . .

it's hungry!

"TYRANT LIZARD KING"
Tyrannosaurus rex
(predator)

LAST MONTH'S LOSERS!

Triceratops skull

HEIGHT	20 feet
LENGTH	40 feet
WEIGHT	8 tons
WEAPON	4-foot jaw
SPEED	10-25 mph

GRRR! IN IT TO WIN IT!

T. rex skull

In this corner—T. rex! It's big, it's brawny, it's a hardheaded, bone-crunching, biting machine.

ROUND ONE

T. rex goes for Triceratops's neck. One powerful bite, and Triceratops would be on the ground.

ROUND TWO

But Triceratops isn't out of this fight yet! It tries to spear T. rex with its deadly horns. Oooh . . . just missed!

10

event!

GO T. REX!

VS.

"THREE-HORNED FACE" Triceratops
(prey)

HEIGHT	7 feet
LENGTH	30 feet
WEIGHT	6 tons
WEAPON	3-foot horns
SPEED	15 mph

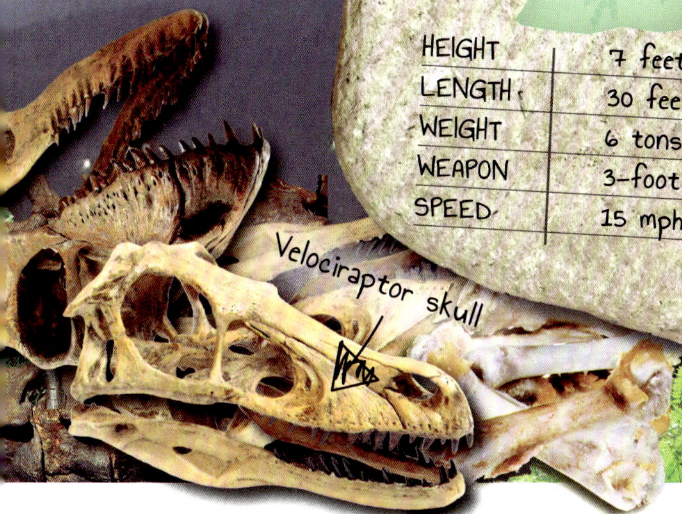

Velociraptor skull

it's meaty!

YOU'RE GOING DOWN!

On this side—Triceratops! It's only half T. rex's size, but it's sturdy on its feet and has three stabbing horns for defense.

Match your stickers to the pictures.

ROUND THREE

T. rex bashes with its hard head. Ooof! Sturdy Triceratops stumbles but stays up.

ROUND FOUR

T. rex gives up. Triceratops wins! T. rex will have to find smaller or weaker prey instead!

11

Let's stick

pterosaur

Don't want to be eaten? Hang with the crowd. Many plant-eaters lived in herds to protect themselves. It's harder for predators to pick off a victim when everybody is bunched together. Hey, you! In the back! No stragglers!

> NYAH, NYAH! WE HAVE REALLY SHARP TEETH!

Packs of Velociraptors would follow a herd of plant-eaters, looking for the weakest one to make it into their next meal. Add stickers to make a raptor army.

← **VELOCIRAPTOR VS.**

together

BIG CLUES that dinos lived in herds:

Lots of fossils of the same kind of dino have been found in one place. Maybe they died together. SPOOKY!

Groups of fossilized nests and eggs suggest that some dino moms-to-be met up.

Matching footprints, all headed the same way, show herds of dinos traveling together.

Barapasaurus

BACK OFF, BUDDY! WE HAVE . . . UH . . . BEAKS.

YEAH, YOU SAID IT!

PROTOCERATOPS

Protoceratops was big. But it was SLOW! Its only defense: a hornlike beak. Add some more stickers and wish these dinos good luck. One of them won't make it to the next page.

13

Fossil fever

Dinosaurs are long gone. (Phew!) So how do we know what they looked like? From fossils! Fossils are the last traces of animals and plants that lived millions of years ago.

How do you dig up a fossil? Very carefully. Scientists might use paintbrushes. Picks. Hammers. Or even bombs, to remove top layers of rock!

Meet some fossil experts. They are called **PALEONTOLOGISTS.**

Top 5

Mary Anning found fossils in England starting in 1811.

Othniel Charles Marsh discovered and named 80 dinos in the late 1800s . . .

. . . and his American rival, Edward Drinker Cope, found and named 56 dinos.

American Barnum Brown discovered the first T. rex fossil in 1902.

Dong Zhiming is a great fossil hunter in China. He's still finding more!

HIP BONE

LEG BONE

Imagine YOU'RE a great paleontologist. Use your stickers to put together the dino skeleton you've found.

14

Light bones, long legs?
Looks fast! And check
out those teeth! This
dinosaur would eat
pretty much anything!

Giant skeleton, huge jaws,
lethal-looking teeth. And
look at those tiny arms!

BACKBONE

A beak? Maybe it ate
like a duck. And quacked
like a duck. But it WASN'T
a duck. And what's that
crest on its head?

SKULL

**ARM
BONE**

Who's who?

The skeletons on these two pages belong
to these three dinosaurs. Can you match
the dinos and their fossils?

Tyrannosaurus rex   Heterodontosaurus   Lambeosaurus

ISBN 978-0-545-63627-8

10 9 8 7 6 5 4 3 2 1   14 15 16 17 18

Printed in Malaysia   106
First edition, January 2014

Dino names

Allosaurus AL-oh-SORE-uss	**Carnotaurus** KAR-noh-TORE-uss	**Eoraptor** EE-oh-RAP-tor	**Microraptor** MY-croh-RAP-tor	**Triceratops** try-SERR-uh-tops
Amargasaurus ah-MARG-ah-SORE-uss	**Coelophysis** SEE-low-FYE-siss	**Gallimimus** gal-li-MY-muss	**Oviraptor** OH-vee-RAP-tor	**Troödon** TROH-oh-don
Ankylosaurus ang-KIE-loh-SORE-uss	**coelurosaur** see-LUR-oh-sore	**Giganotosaurus** GEE-gan-NO-toh-SORE-uss	**Protoceratops** proh-toh-SERR-uh-tops	**Tyrannosaurus rex** ty-RAN-oh-SORE-uss rex
Apatosaurus ah-PAT-oh-SORE-uss	**Compsognathus** komp-sog-NAYTH-uss	**Herrerasaurus** he-RAIR-ah-SORE-uss	**Pteranodon** terr-AN-oh-don	**Velociraptor** vell-OSS-ee-RAP-tor
Archaeopteryx ar-key-OP-ter-iks	**Corythosaurus** kor-ITH-oh-SORE-uss	**Heterodontosaurus** HET-er-oh-DON-toh-SORE-uss	**pterosaur** TERR-oh-sore	**Vulcanodon** vull-KAN-oh-don
Argentinosaurus AR-jen-TEEN-oh-SORE-uss	**Deinonychus** dy-NON-ick-uss	**Iguanodon** ig-WAHN-oh-don	**Spinosaurus** SPY-no-SORE-uss	
Barapasaurus bah-RAH-pah-SORE-uss	**Diplodocus** di-PLOD-oh-kuss	**Lambeosaurus** LAM-bee-oh-SORE-uss	**Stegosaurus** STEG-oh-SORE-uss	

Image credits